I0938982

WE

ARE

ALL

DOTS

A Big Plan for a Better World

Giancarlo Macri
Carolina Zanotti

UNIVERSE

Hi!
I'm a dot.

Can you see me?
I'm down here.

•

I don't live alone.
I have friends.

And my friends have friends.
And their friends have friends.

There are lots
and lots of us
on this page.

Life is good. We have housing,

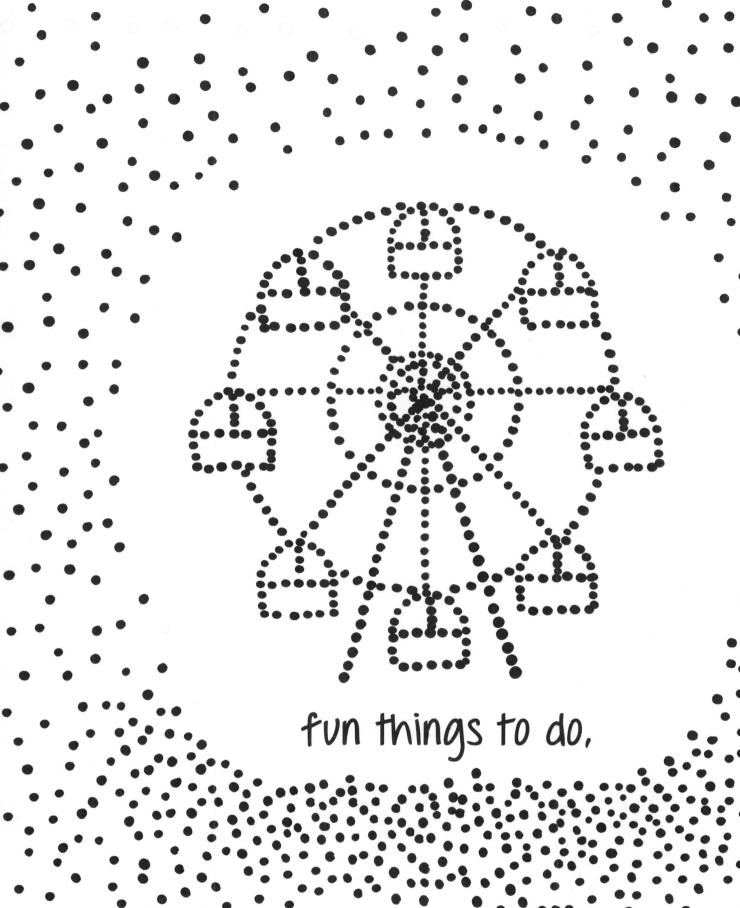

fun things to do,

and food to eat.

o

Hi.
I'm a dot.

Can you see me?
I'm up here.

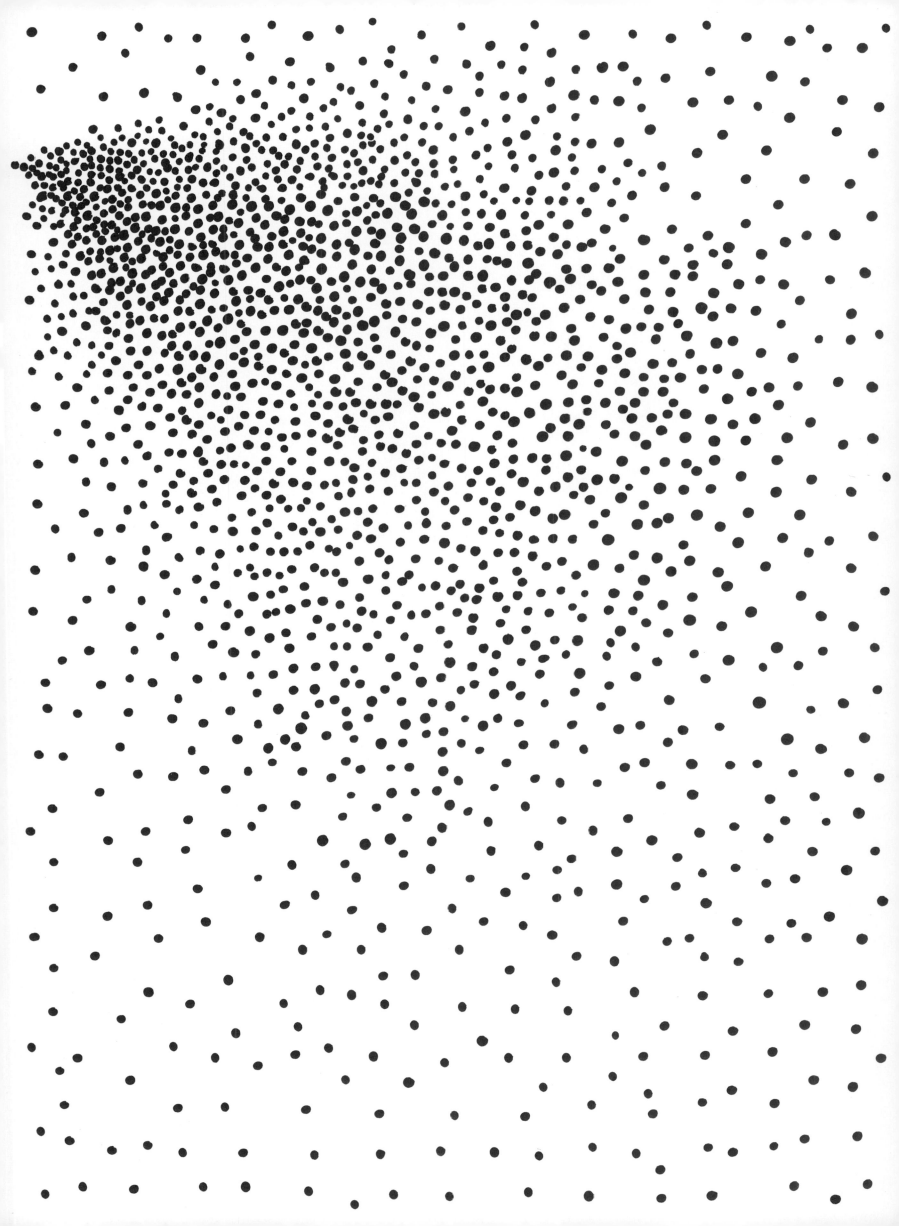

There are lots and lots of us too.

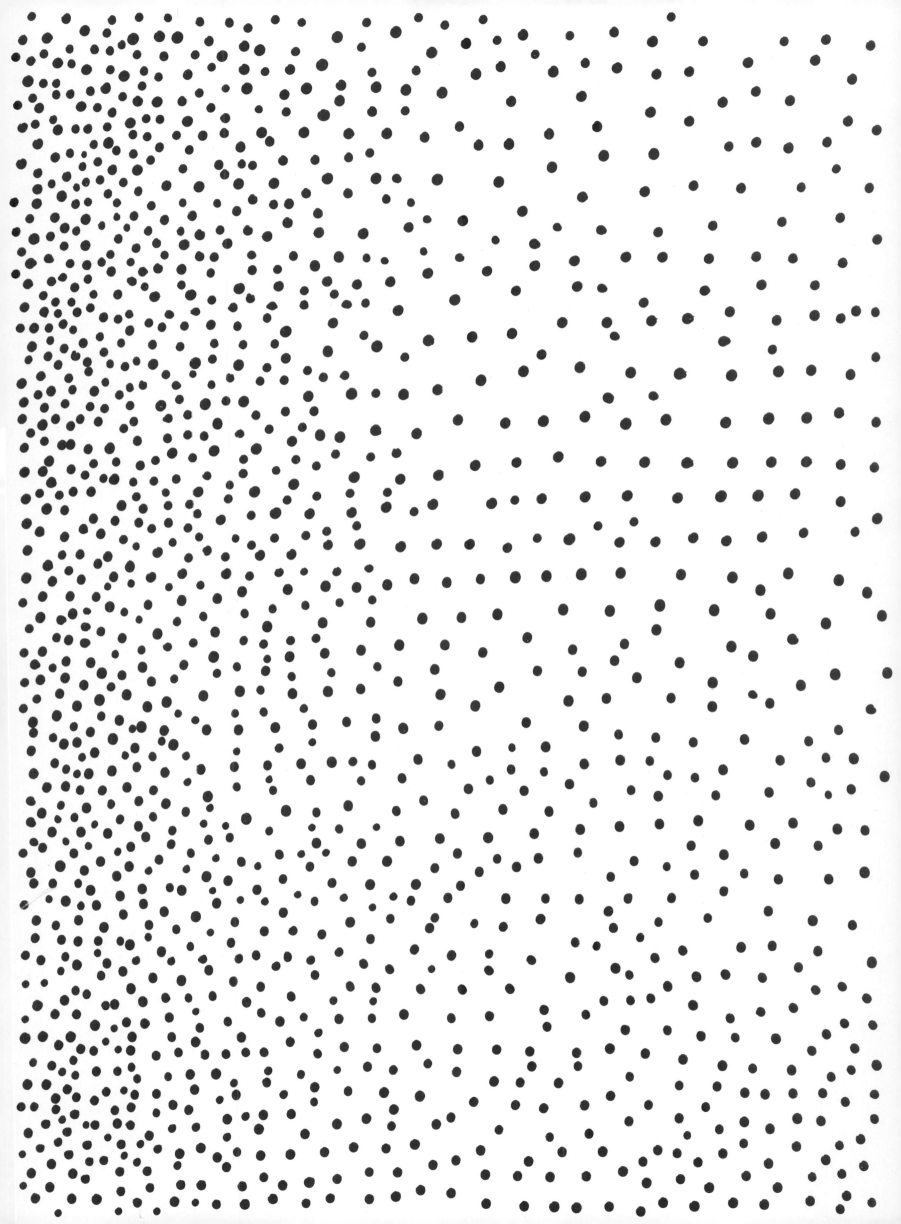

Over here, life isn't so good.
We have no housing,
no fun things to do,
no food to eat.

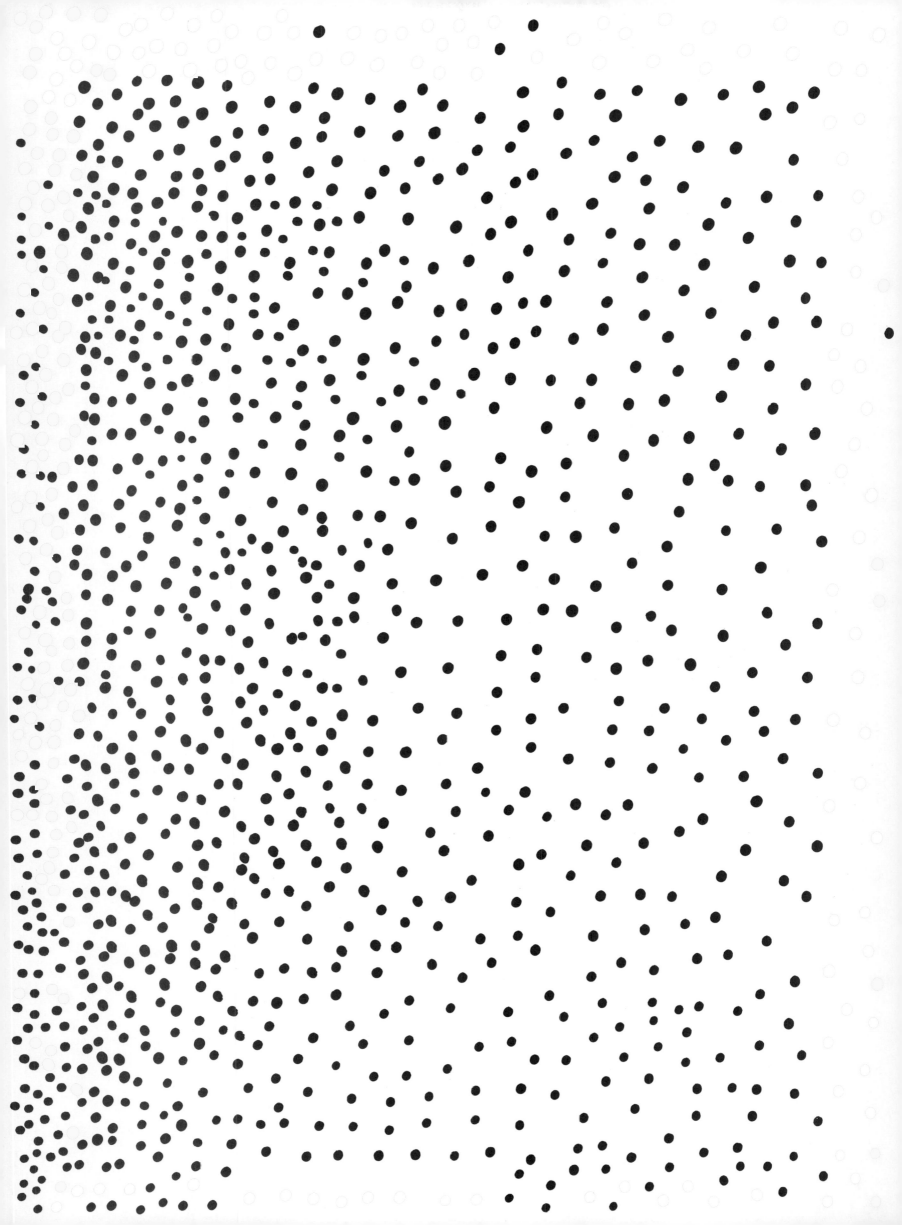

we'd like to come
over to your page.

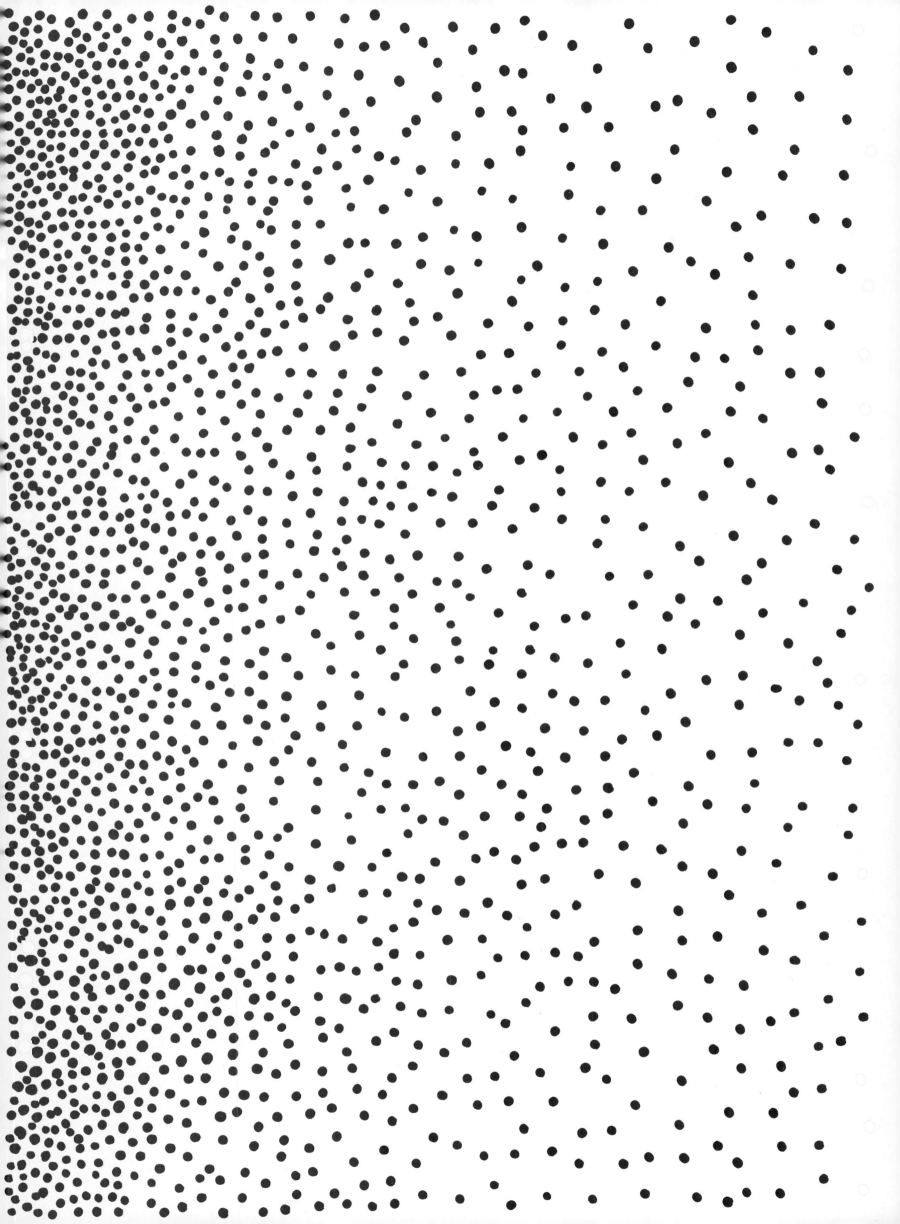

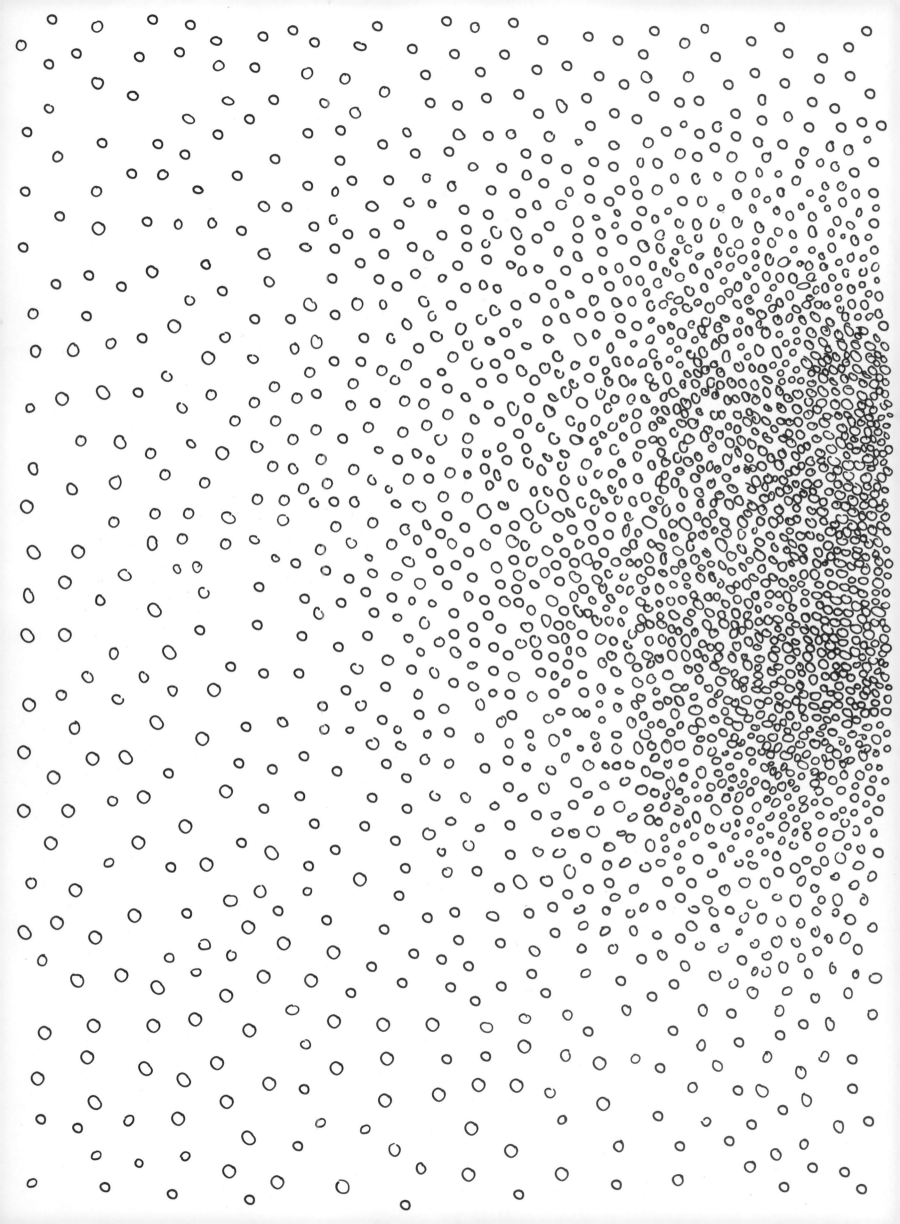

Wait! We have to decide if we will
let you come over to our page.

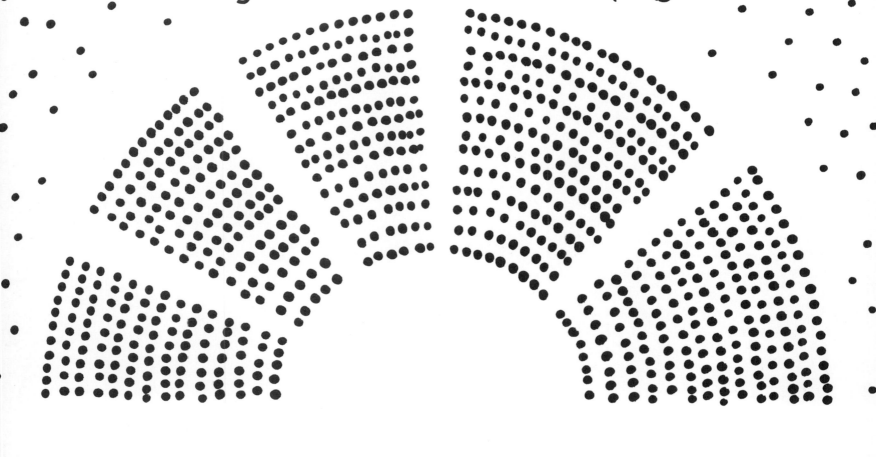

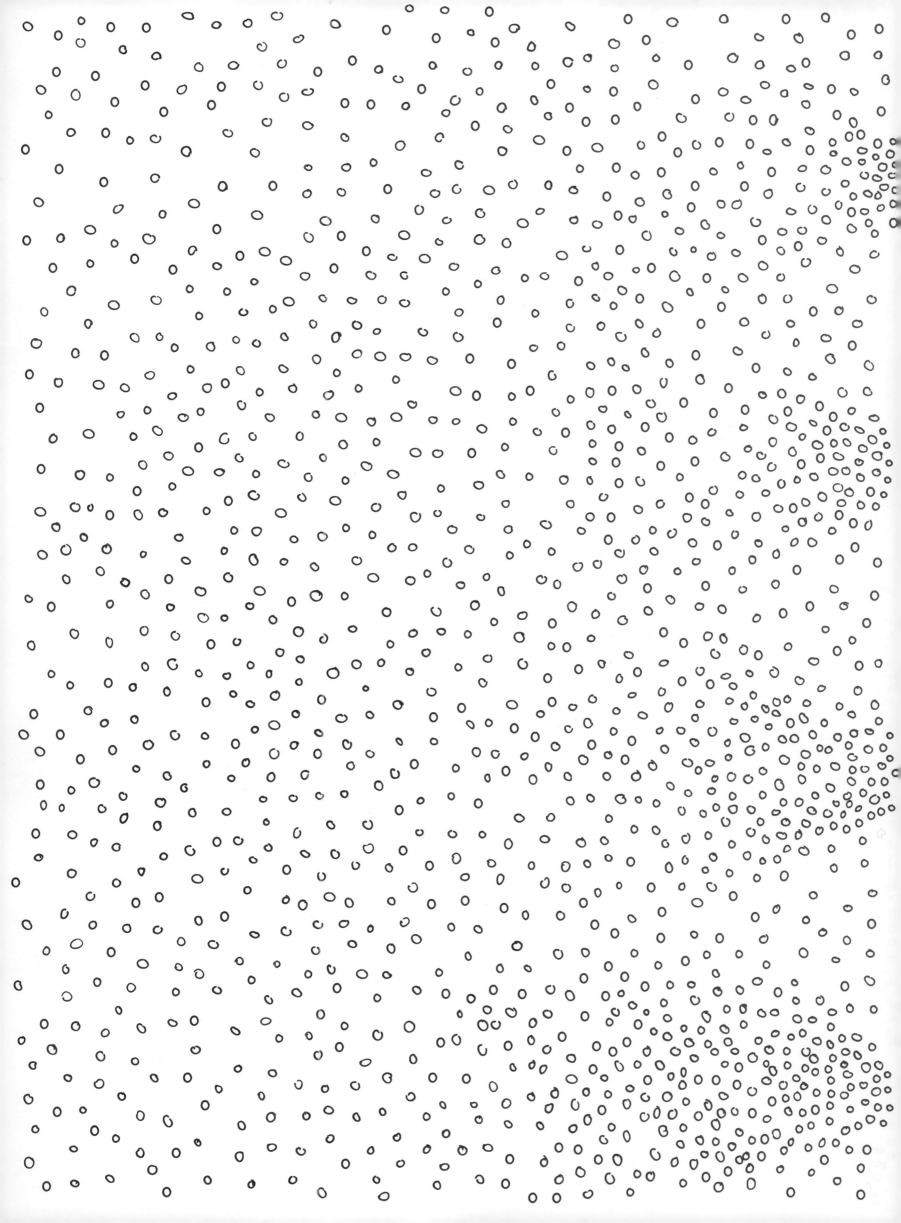

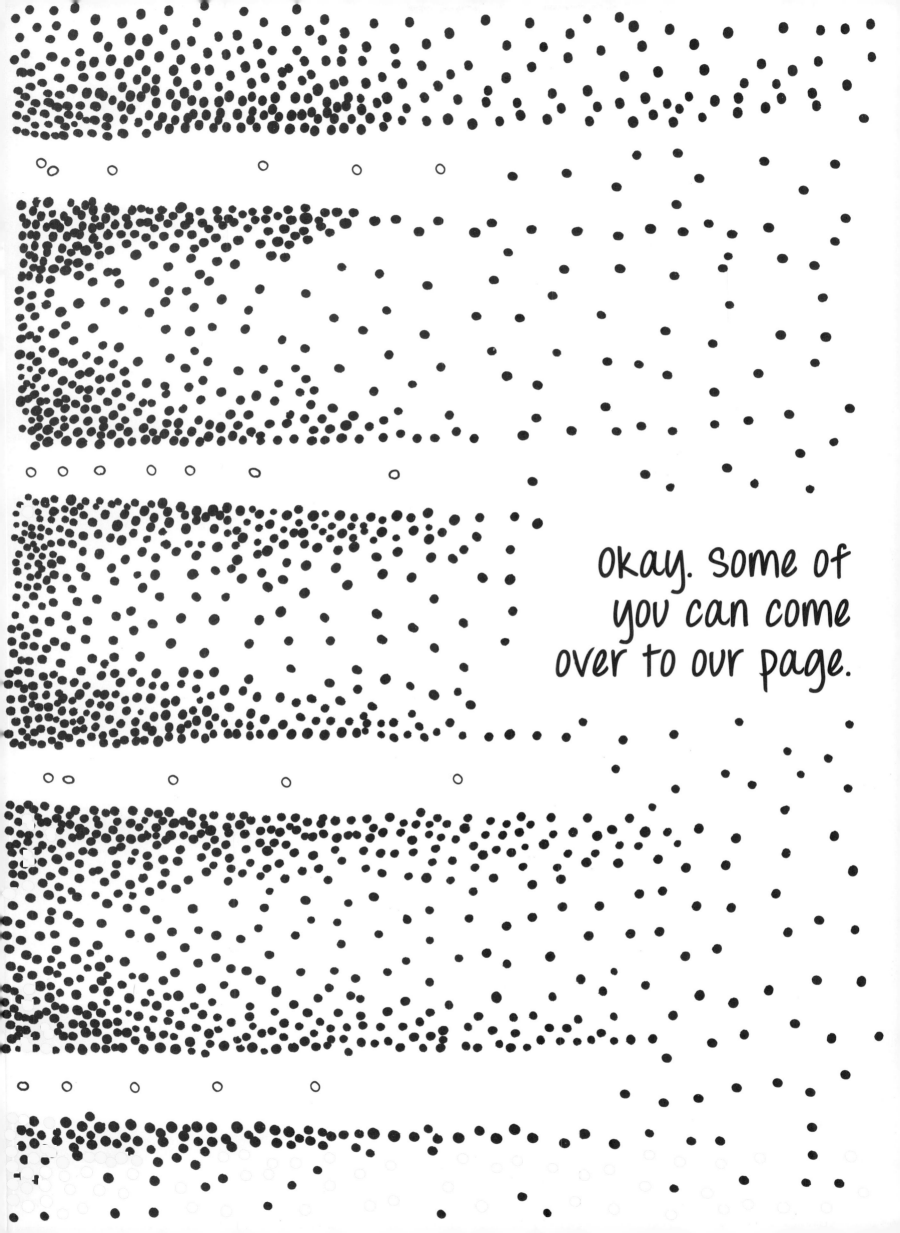

Okay. Some of
you can come
over to our page.

Stop! That's enough!
We can't all fit ...
on this page.

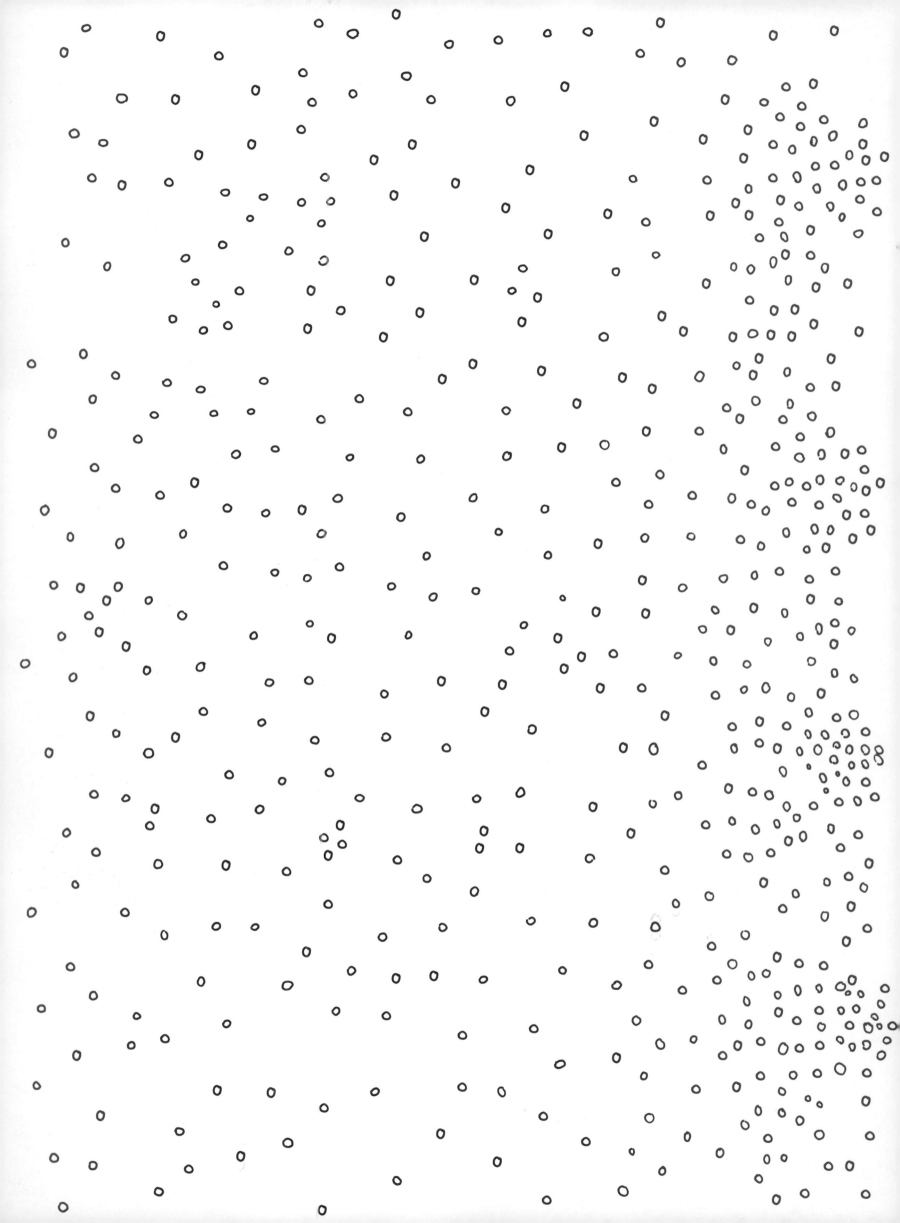

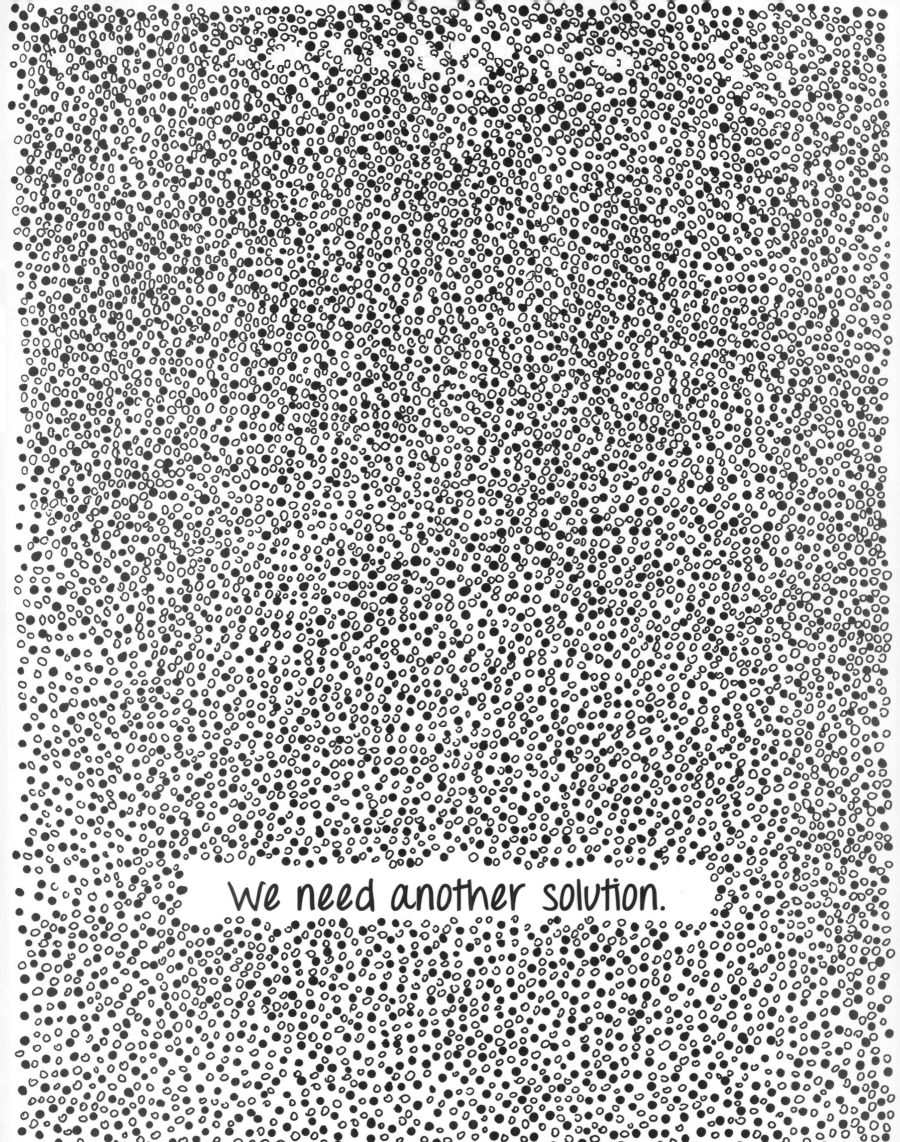

We need another solution.

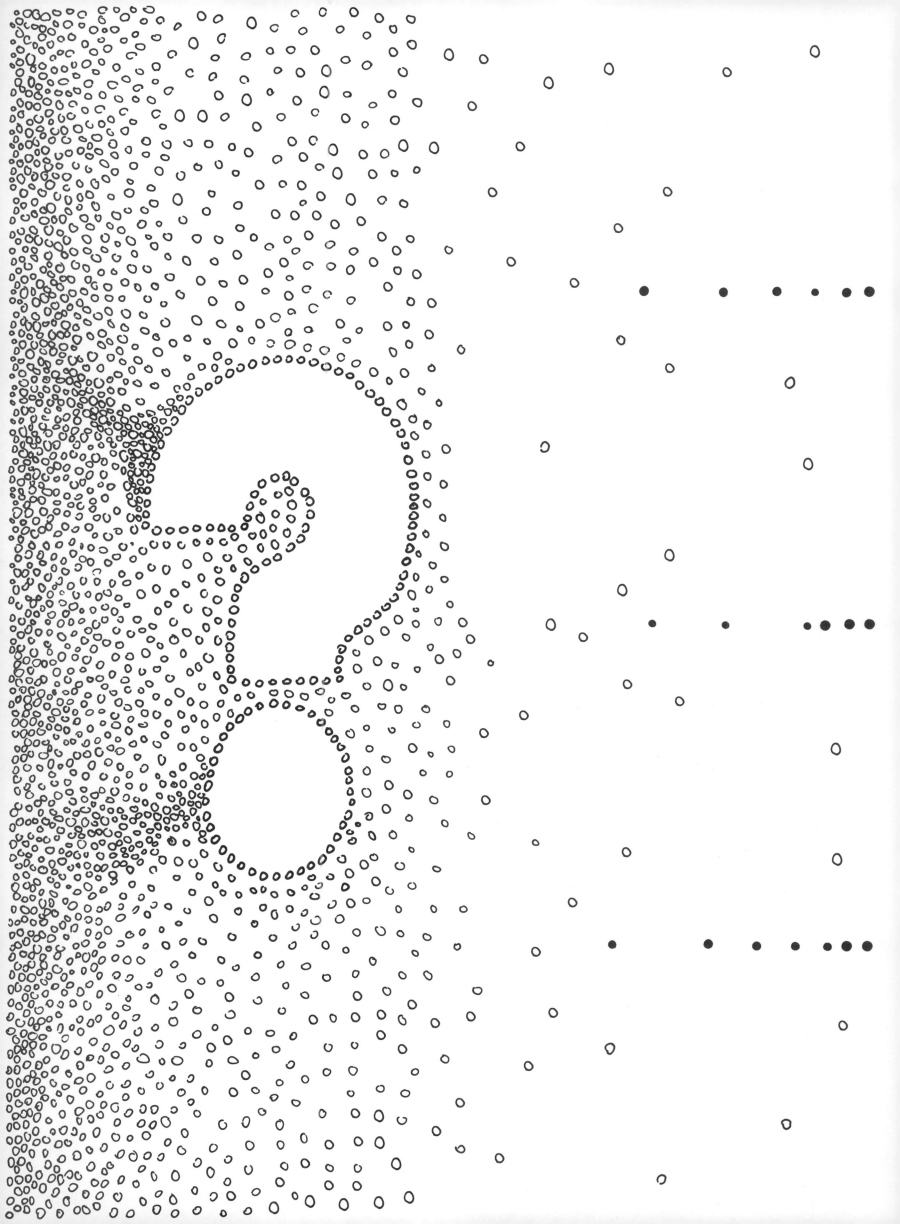

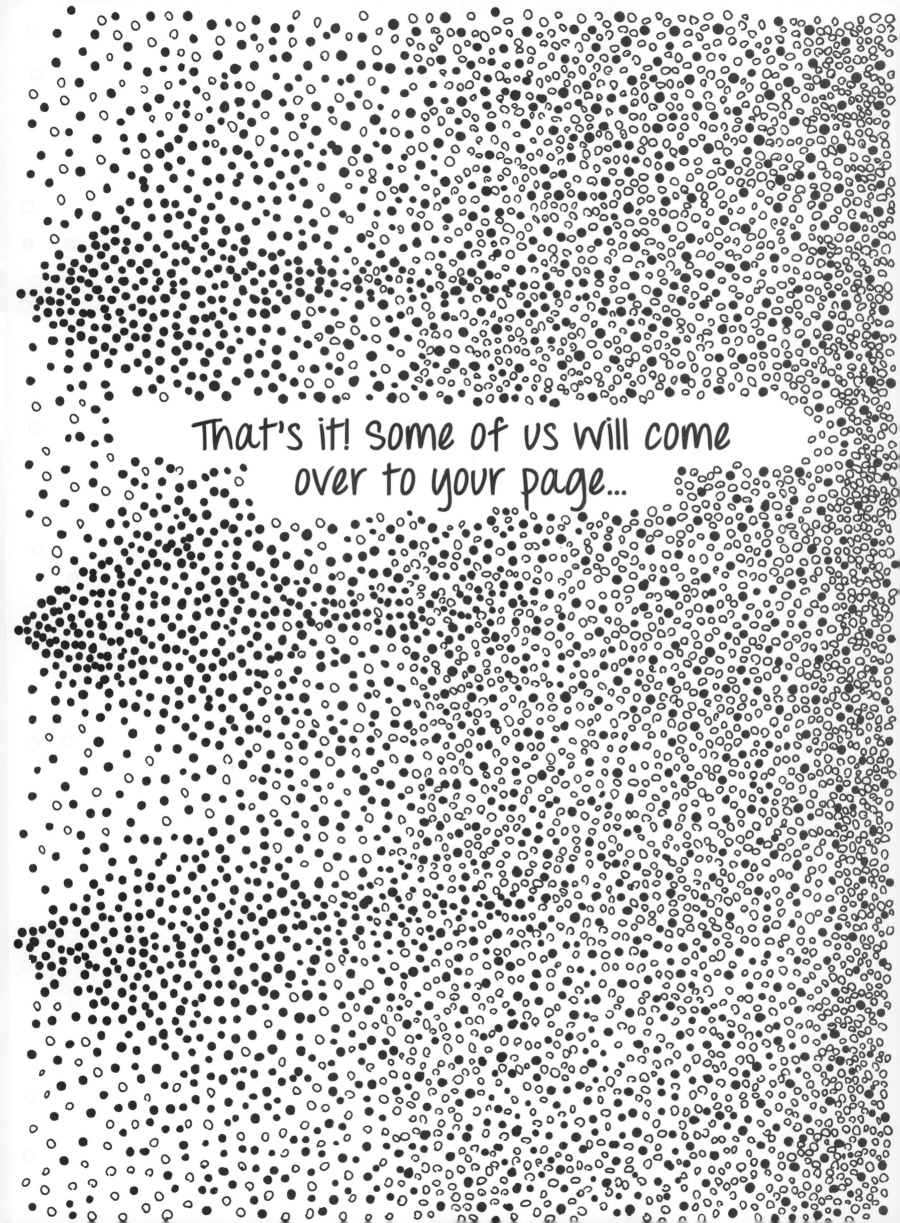

That's it! Some of us will come over to your page...

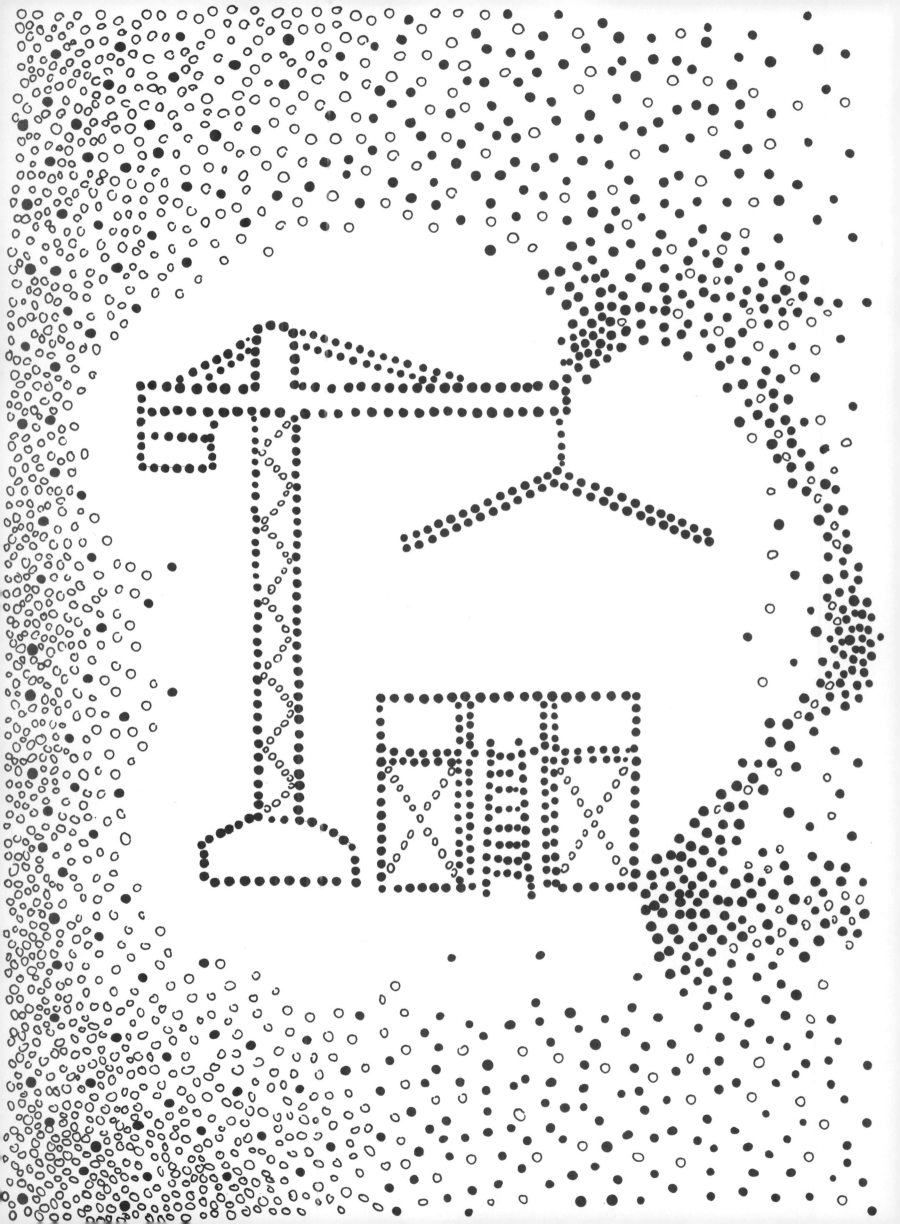

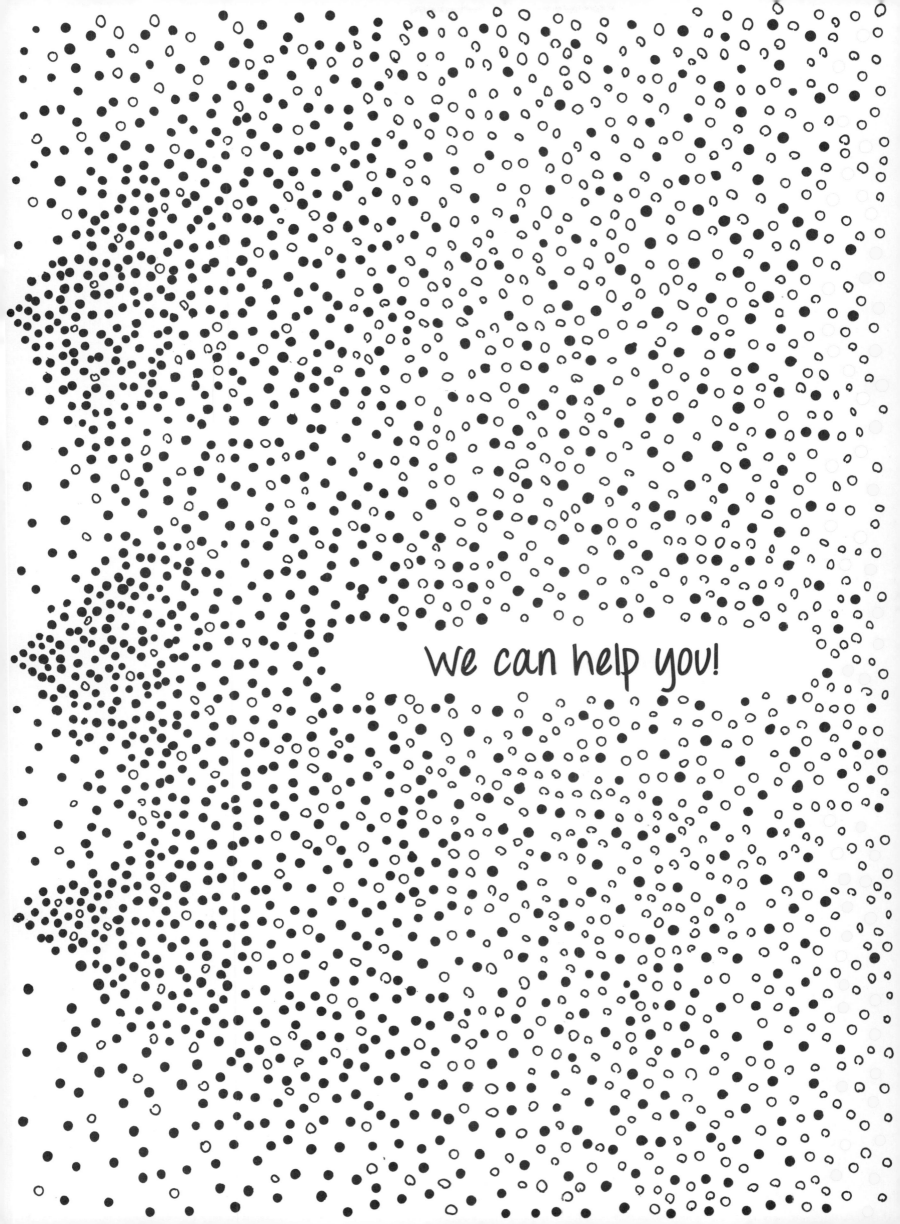

Together, we can

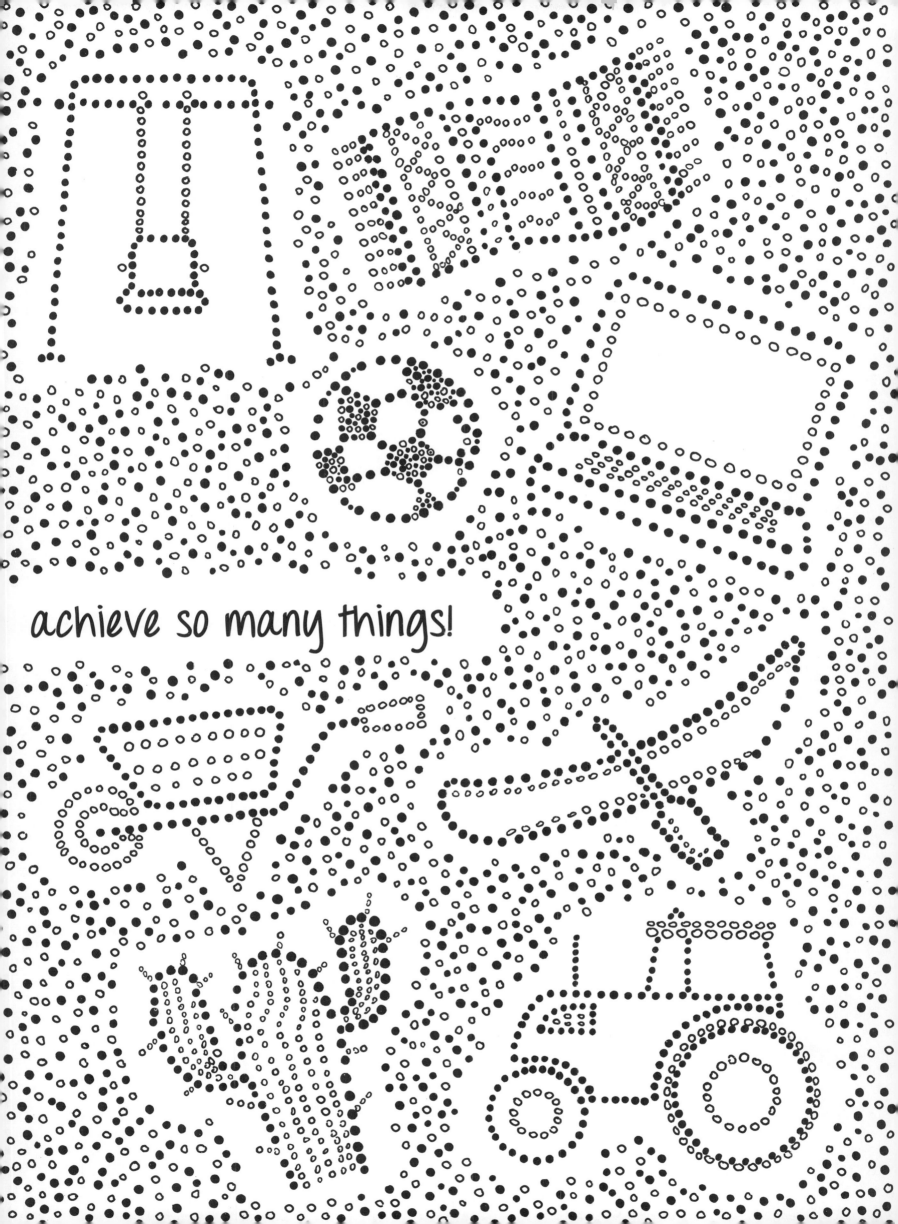

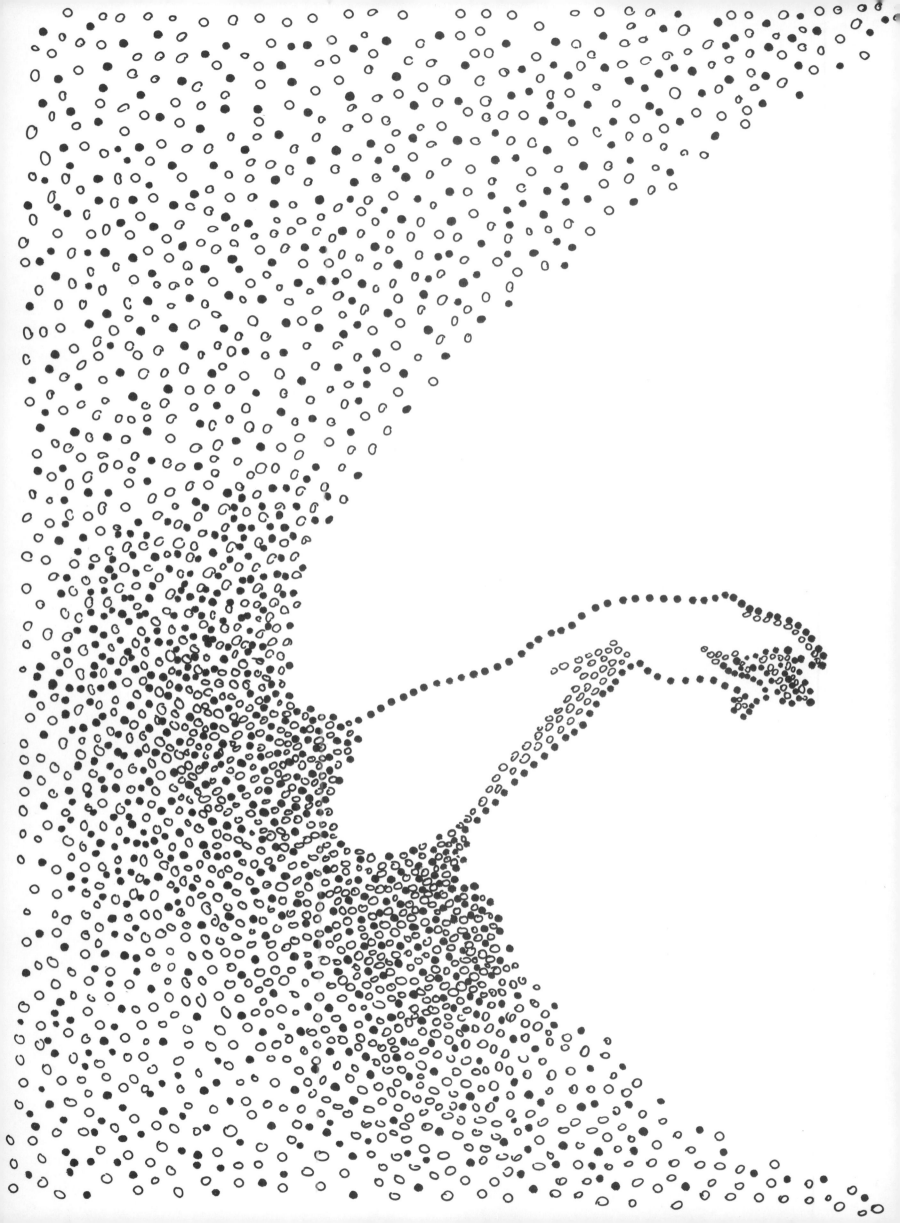

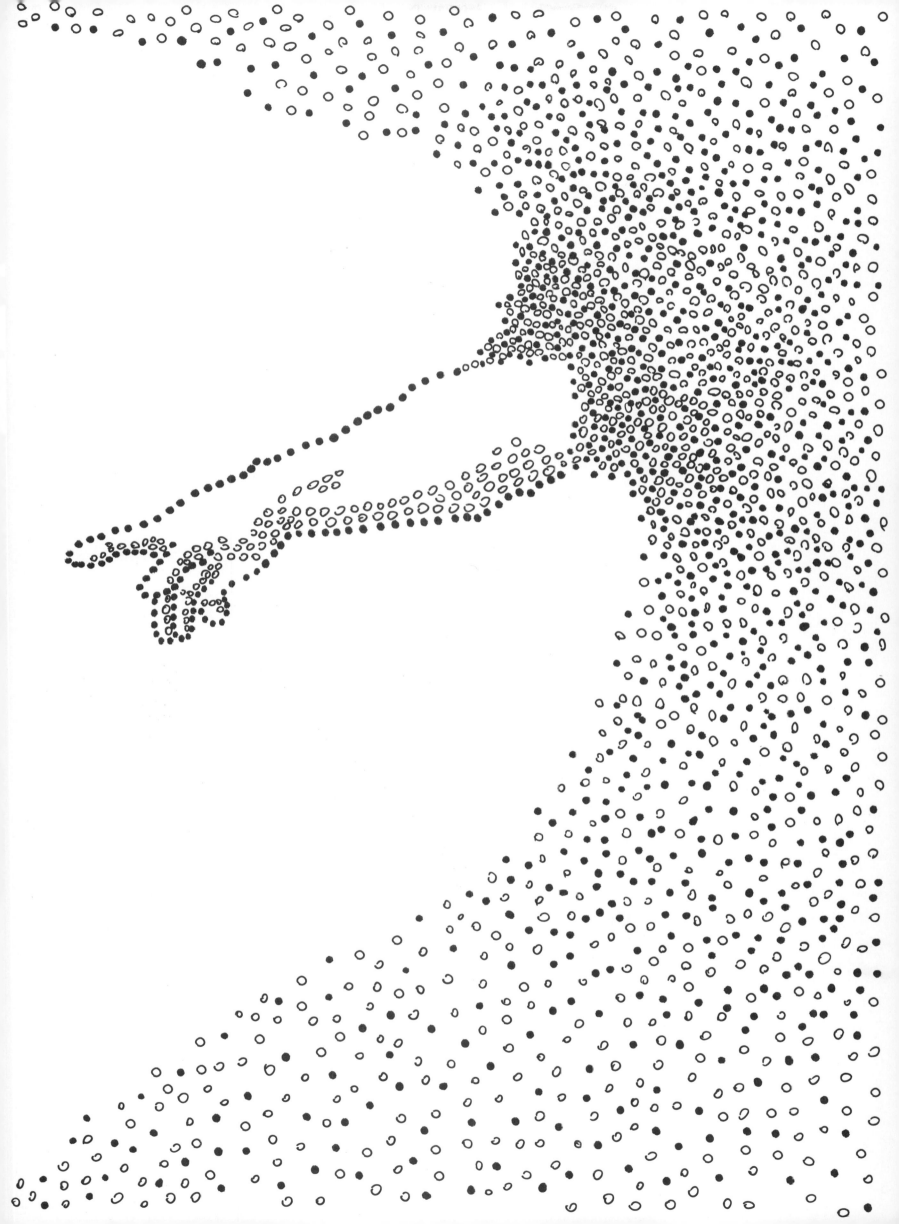

Hi, I'm a dot.

●

Hi, I'm a dot.

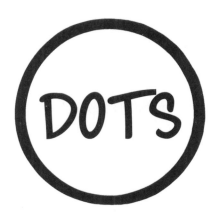

Giancarlo Macrì, actor and musician, was a founding member of the Banda Osiris, a legendary group active in theater, television, radio, and publishing, as well as the author of prize-winning film soundtracks. He has published several children's books.

Carolina Zanotti is a journalist specializing in music and theater. A lover of figurative arts, she has written several children's stories.

Texts and illustrations: Giancarlo Macrì and Carolina Zanotti
Graphic design: Clara Zanotti
US Jacket Design: Kayleigh Jankowski

First published in the United States of America in 2018 by Universe Publishing
A Division of
Rizzoli International Publications, Inc.
300 Park Avenue South
New York, NY 10010
www.rizzoliusa.com

Originally published in Italian in 2015 by Nuinui, an imprint of Snake SA, Switzerland
© 2015 Snake SA

2018 2019 2020 2021 / 10 9 8 7 6 5 4 3 2 1
ISBN: 978-0-7893-3429-9
Library of Congress Control Number: 2017956285

Printed in China